9/02

North American
Historical Atlases

EXPLORING
THE NEW
WORLD

A 1562 picture of the harbor of Lisbon, Portugal's capital, crowded with ships bound for the Americas.

North American Historical Atlases

EXPLORING THE NEW WORLD

Rebecca Stefoff

BENCHMARK BOOKS

MARSHALL CAVENDISH
NEW YORK

Benchmark Books
Marshall Cavendish Corporation
99 White Plains Road
Tarrytown, New York 10591

• • •

Library of Congress Cataloging-in-Publication Data
Stefoff, Rebecca, date.
Exploring the New World/Rebecca Stefoff
p. cm—(North American Historical Atlases)
Includes bibliographical references and index.
Summary: Traces the exploration of America from the arrival of Asian hunters
in Alaska more than 15,000 years ago to the English and French settlers in early 1600s.
ISBN 0-7614-1056-2 (lib.bdg.)
1. America—Discovery and exploration—Juvenile literature.   2. America—Discovery and exploration—
Maps—Juvenile literature.   3. Explorers—America—History—Juvenile literature.   [America—Discovery
and exploration.   2. America—Discovery and exploration—Maps.   3. Explorers.]   I. Title.
E101.S835   2001   99-052973   970.01—dc21

• • •

Printed in Hong Kong
3 5 7 8 6 4 2

• • •

Book Designer: Judith Turziano
Photo Researcher: Matthew Dudley

• • •

CREDITS
Front cover: *Corbis-Bettmann*—World Map circa 1570.
Back cover: *Giraudon/Art Resource, NY*—Painting by Theodore Jean Antoine Gudin.
Jacques Cartier discovers the St. Lawrence River in 1535.

The photographs and maps in this book are used by permission and through the courtesy of:
Archive Photos: 35, 42 (top), 42 (bottom). *The Beinecke Rare Book and Manuscript Library at
Yale University*: 22. *Corbis-Bettmann*: 19, 20, 23, 25, 28, 31 (bottom), 31 (top), 32, 37, 40.
Giraudon/Art Resource, NY: 2-3, 7, 10, 16, 21. *The Library of Congress Maps Division*: 41.
Photo Researchers, Inc: Lawrence Migdale, 12; George Gerster, 14. *Rare Book Division, The
New York Public Library, Astor, Lenox, and Tilden Foundations*: 30, 43.

Contents

Chapter One

THE FIRST EXPLORERS

The first explorers of North America were not just visiting—they were the first people to live there. They were the ancestors of today's Native Americans.

The Land Bridge

The world has not always looked the way it looks today. From 100,000 until 15,000 years ago, the Earth was in the grip of an Ice Age. Great ice sheets covered much of northern Europe and North America. So much water was frozen into these **glaciers** that the sea was 300 feet (91 meters) lower than its present level. Shorelines were very different from those we see on our globes and maps.

On today's globes and maps, Siberia in northeastern Asia and Alaska in northwestern North America reach toward each other as though the continents were trying to link hands. A narrow arm of the Pacific Ocean called the Bering Strait runs between them, keeping them apart. But during the Ice Age the ocean was too shallow to flow through the Bering Strait. Siberia and Alaska were joined by a wide belt of treeless, gently rolling land—a land bridge. Modern scientists call that land bridge Beringia.

Beringia must have been much like Siberia—a windswept place with long, harsh winters and brief summers. The Siberian **steppe-tundra** was home to cold-loving animals such as woolly **mammoths**, steppe bison, and caribou. Eventually these animals roamed eastward into Beringia. So did the human hunters who followed them. And one day a group of these ancient hunters reached Alaska and became the first people to enter North America.

Filling an Empty World

Most scientists believe that people entered Beringia sometime between 18,000 or 25,000 years ago, but no one knows exactly when they arrived in Alaska. We do know that human beings were living in central Alaska at the end of the Ice Age, about 15,000 years ago. As the ice sheets melted and the seas rose, Beringia disappeared beneath the waves. The people in Alaska were cut off from the Old World, and the New World belonged to them and their descendants.

At first a wall of ice kept them from moving very far into that world. The Ice Age glaciers covered southern Alaska and all of what is now Canada. Even if, as some **geologists** believe, there were ice-free pockets or corridors between the ice sheets, these would have been bleak and bitter places, poor homes for animals or people. But when the ice sheets began to shrink, the land grew warmer and more fertile. Animals and hunters moved south. By 10,000 years ago humans were living throughout the Americas.

Early Hunters

Scientists call the first inhabitants of North America Paleoindians, which means "ancient Indians." Today experts search eagerly for

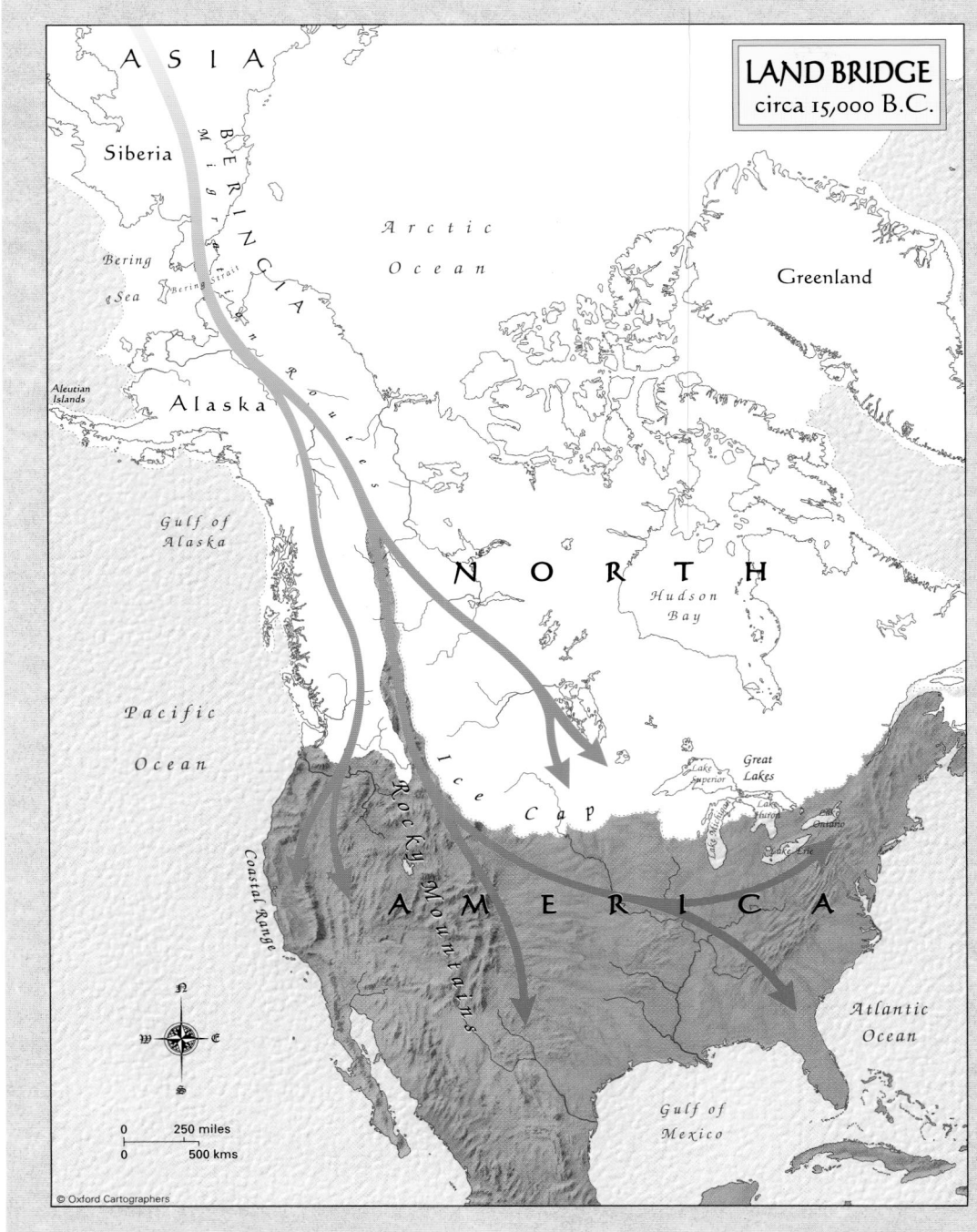

LAND BRIDGE
circa 15,000 B.C.

ASIA

Siberia

Bering Sea

Aleutian Islands

Alaska

Gulf of Alaska

Pacific Ocean

BERINGIA

Migration Routes

Arctic Ocean

Greenland

NORTH

Hudson Bay

Ice Cap

Coastal Range

Rocky Mountains

AMERICA

Lake Superior

Great Lakes

Lake Michigan

Lake Huron

Lake Erie

Lake Ontario

Atlantic Ocean

Gulf of Mexico

0   250 miles
0   500 kms

© Oxford Cartographers

Some of the biggest questions in prehistoric studies involve the settling of the Americas. Although the full story of how the first people came to the Americas is not yet known, scientists know that the distant ancestors of the Native Americans came from northern Asia across a land bridge called Beringia. These roving hunters had reached North America by 15,000 years ago—but could they have arrived long before that? A few archaeological sites, including some as far from Beringia as South America's Andes Mountains, hint at a human presence in the Americas as early as 40,000 years ago, but these sites are still the subject of much scientific study and debate.

Archaeologists identify Paleoindian cultures by the few objects they left behind,
such as these 10,000-year-old spear points found in Wyoming.

traces of their presence—and sometimes argue over the age of those traces. Most of them do agree that Fort Rock Cave in Oregon contains Paleoindian stone tools that may be 14,000 years old. These are among the oldest definite human traces in North America.

Around 9500 B.C. a new Paleoindian culture emerged on the Great Plains. **Archaeologists** call it the Clovis culture because it is recognized by carefully made stone spear points first found in Clovis, New Mexico.

The Clovis people lived in small groups that traveled for most of the year, gathering wild plant foods and following herds of game. They were daring hunters, able to tackle the largest animals of the time, and skilled toolmakers who could work lumps of stone into fine, sharp points and blades.

The Clovis culture flourished for 500 years and then disappeared. Scientists are not sure why the Clovis people vanished, but they know that other hunting-and-gathering cultures took their place. At Folsom, New Mexico, scientists have found stone spear points with the bones of bison from 9000 B.C. In the centuries that followed, other bison hunters roamed the Great Plains, and different kinds of cultures arose elsewhere.

First Communities

In time, some ancient hunter-gatherers formed fixed **settlements**, such as the Adena and Hopewell cultures that flourished along the Ohio River between 1000 B.C. and A.D. 400. After the people of eastern North America learned to grow corn and beans, agriculture gave them a steady food supply and allowed them to create even larger communities, including Cahokia in Illinois and Moundville in Alabama.

Northwestern people settled along rivers and on the ocean coast. They fished, hunted whales and other sea mammals, and built houses of cedar and fir. Many features of early Pacific Northwest life were preserved at Ozette in Washington State, where a mudslide covered a village that dated from before A.D. 1200. Although they lived in a dry region, Southwestern people also practiced agriculture, using clever **irrigation** systems to water their fields. The Hohokam people built a large settlement known as Snaketown on the banks of the Gila River. The ancestors of today's Pueblo Indians, sometimes called the Anasazi, created many-roomed structures at Chaco Canyon, and at Mesa Verde they built houses high above the floor of a canyon, tucked under ledges in the cliff walls and reachable only by ladder.

HUNTERS AND EXTINCT ANIMALS

 Around the time the Clovis people disappeared, so did their favorite prey, the huge, shaggy mammoths. Other animals, including the camels and giant ground sloths that once lived in North America, also became extinct at that time.

A few scientists claim that the Clovis people hunted the mammoths and other creatures into extinction. Other experts argue that overhunting cannot account for the extinctions that happened all over the world at the end of the Ice Age. They believe that hotter, drier weather and other changing conditions made life increasingly difficult for species that had adapted to Ice Age conditions. But perhaps human hunters, with their ability to kill large numbers of animals, tipped the balance in favor of extinction.

*Cliff dwellings like this one in New Mexico's Bandelier National Monument are
found throughout the region where Colorado, Utah, New Mexico, and Arizona meet.
Once they were home to the ancestors of today's Native American Pueblo peoples.*

The Native Americans

By the 1400s about four and a half million Native Americans lived in North America in hundreds of separate groups, which we now call nations or tribes. These nations fell into ten larger categories called culture groups. The tribes within each culture group shared certain traits. They used the same kinds of

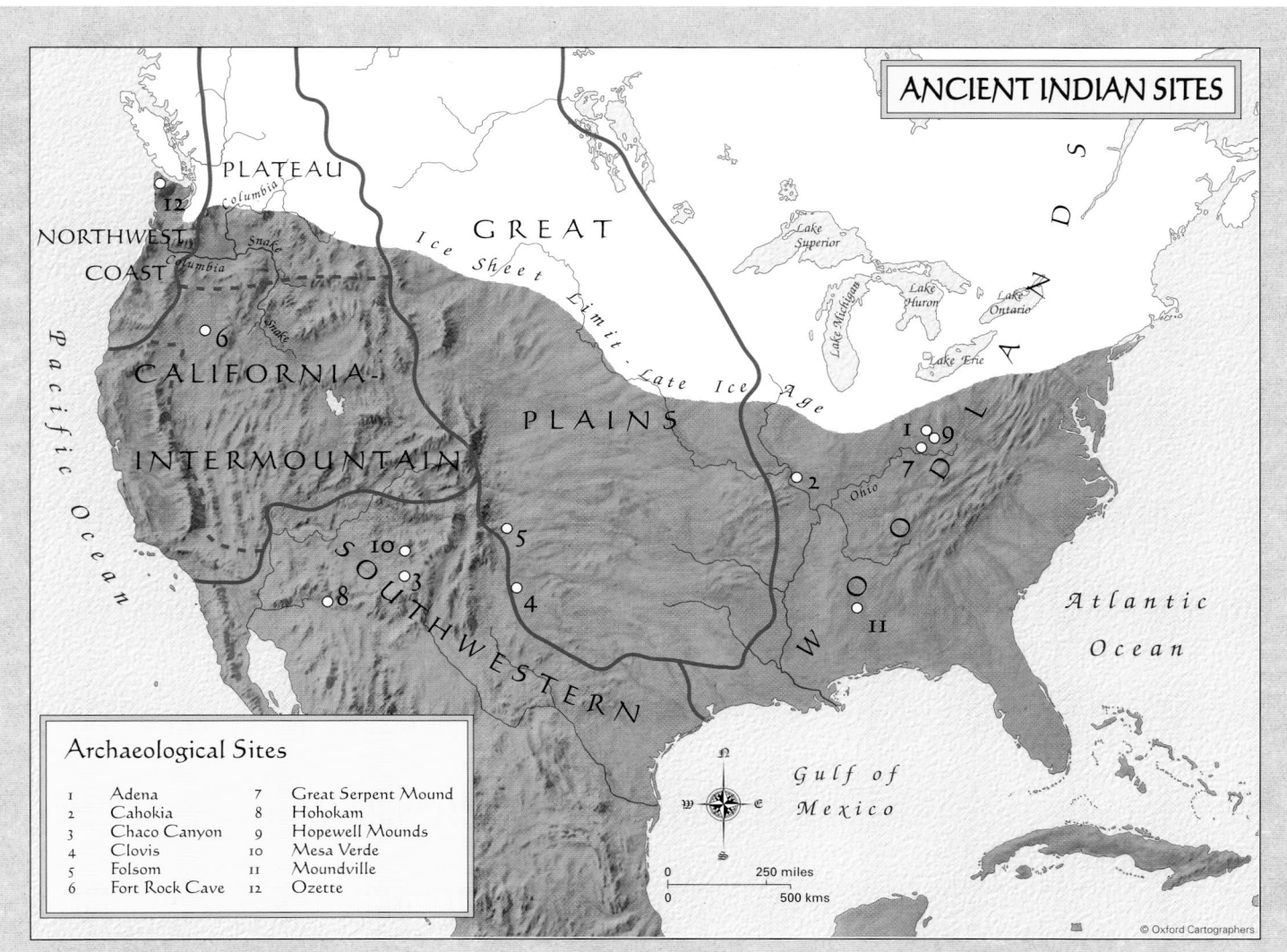

ANCIENT INDIAN SITES

PLATEAU

NORTHWEST COAST

CALIFORNIA-INTERMOUNTAIN

GREAT

PLAINS

SOUTHWESTERN

WOODLANDS

Pacific Ocean

Atlantic Ocean

Gulf of Mexico

Lake Superior
Lake Michigan
Lake Huron
Lake Ontario
Lake Erie

Columbia
Snake
Ohio

Ice Sheet Limit - Late Ice Age

Archaeological Sites

1	Adena	7	Great Serpent Mound
2	Cahokia	8	Hohokam
3	Chaco Canyon	9	Hopewell Mounds
4	Clovis	10	Mesa Verde
5	Folsom	11	Moundville
6	Fort Rock Cave	12	Ozette

0   250 miles
0   500 kms

© Oxford Cartographers

As they rose and fell over thousands of years, the early North American cultures created artifacts, or human-made objects. Some of these artifacts have survived to the present day. From the stone spear points found at Clovis, which are about 10,000 years old, to the much more recently buried village at Ozette, they tell us something about how ancient people lived, worked, fought, and traded. The Native American cultures did not develop written languages, however, so modern researchers must rely on careful, educated guesswork when trying to reconstruct the past.

THE MYSTERIES OF THE MOUNDS

 The people of Adena, Hopewell, Cahokia, and other places in central North America were mound builders. Using only simple digging tools and baskets, they shaped earth into pyramids or artificial hills. The average mound at Hopewell is 30 feet (9 meters) high and 100 feet (30 meters) across—and represents about 200,000 hours of earthmoving. Even larger is the Great Serpent Mound in Ohio, which looks like a snake coiled along a ridge with another mound clutched in its jaws.

Ohio's Great Serpent Mound, a relic of the Adena or Hopewell culture, is the world's largest known snake image. It is 20 feet (6 meters) wide and 5 feet (1½ meters) high.

The mounds puzzled European and American explorers and historians. Some suggested that voyagers from Egypt or some other Old World civilization had built these impressive monuments. Today we know that Native Americans built the mounds as burial places for their chiefs and nobles. Many mounds contain trade goods that their builders prized, including pottery, axes, and ornaments of shell and copper.

tools, lived in similar ways, spoke related languages, and perhaps worshiped the same gods. The Arctic and Subarctic culture groups, hunters and fishers, lived in what is now Canada. The culture of the Arctic people, or Inuit, was much like that of their Siberian ancestors. The Inuit possessed skills, such as building snow houses and making waterproof clothing, that helped them survive in North America's most hostile climate.

The Northwest Coast peoples used resources from both forest and sea, building impressive cedar houses and canoes and relying upon salmon as their most important food. The tribes of the Plateau culture group lived farther inland but fished for salmon in rivers such

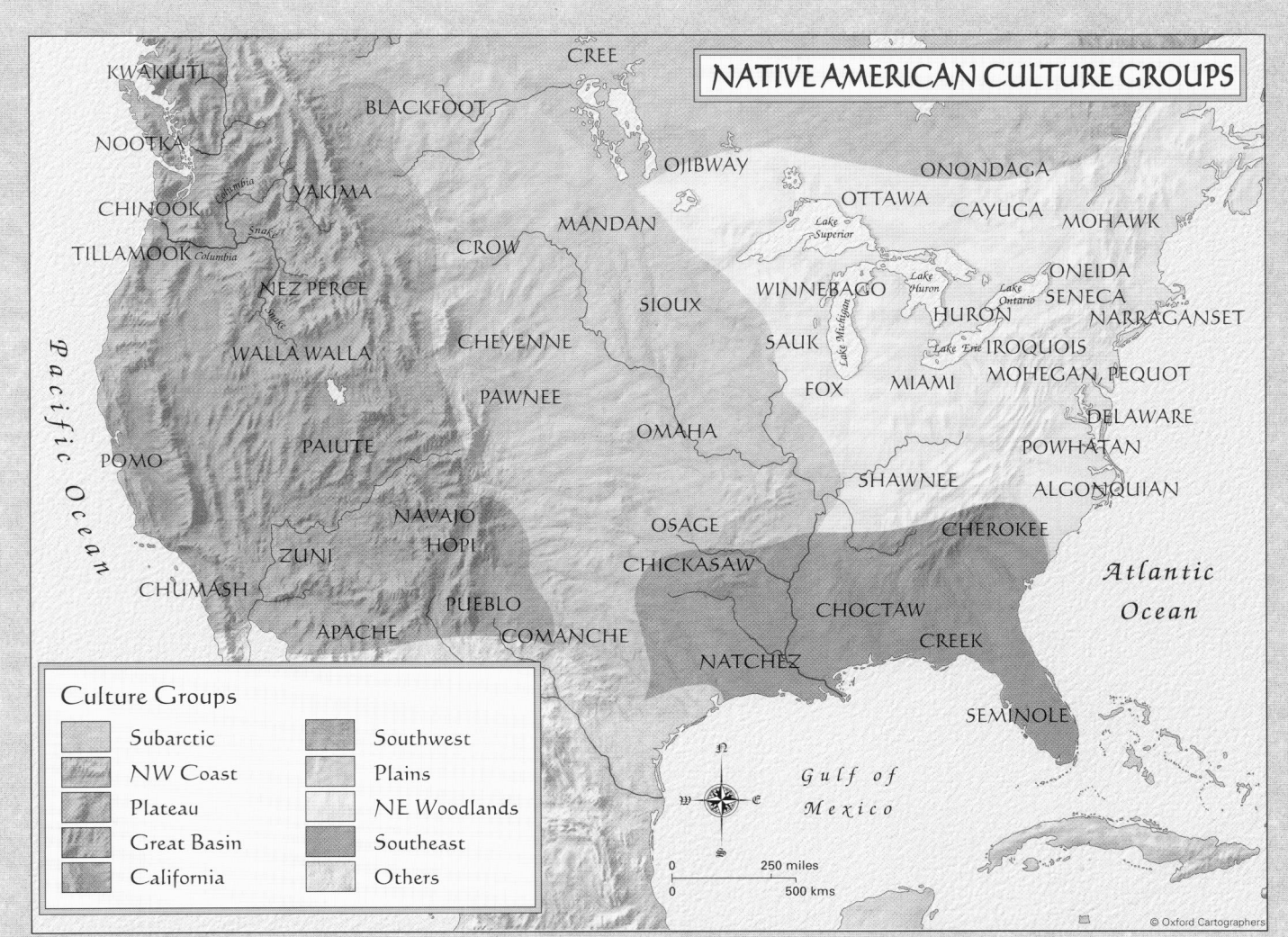

NATIVE AMERICAN CULTURE GROUPS

KWAKIUTL
CREE
BLACKFOOT
NOOTKA
OJIBWAY
ONONDAGA
CHINOOK
YAKIMA
OTTAWA
CAYUGA
MOHAWK
MANDAN
TILLAMOOK
Columbia
CROW
WINNEBAGO
ONEIDA
SENECA
NEZ PERCE
Lake Superior
HURON
NARRAGANSET
SIOUX
Lake Huron
Lake Ontario
WALLA WALLA
CHEYENNE
SAUK
Lake Michigan
IROQUOIS
Lake Erie
MOHEGAN, PEQUOT
PAWNEE
FOX
MIAMI
POMO
PAIUTE
OMAHA
DELAWARE
POWHATAN
SHAWNEE
ALGONQUIAN
NAVAJO
OSAGE
CHEROKEE
HOPI
ZUNI
CHICKASAW
Atlantic Ocean
CHUMASH
CHOCTAW
PUEBLO
APACHE
COMANCHE
CREEK
NATCHEZ
Pacific Ocean
Snake
Columbia
Snake

SEMINOLE

Culture Groups

Subarctic	Southwest
NW Coast	Plains
Plateau	NE Woodlands
Great Basin	Southeast
California	Others

Gulf of Mexico

0   250 miles
0   500 kms

© Oxford Cartographers

By the time Europeans began exploring North America around 1500, the continent's Native American inhabitants had formed a great many distinct nations, or tribes. This map identifies the major Native American nations and shows approximately where they lived before the coming of the Europeans. Modern anthropologists—scientists who study the similarities and differences among human cultures—divide the nations into culture groups. Each group possessed highly developed skills that enabled it to survive in a particular environment and to make the most of the resources available. The Plateau and Great Basin culture groups were the last to be encountered by the Europeans.

Europeans of the sixteenth and seventeenth centuries drew most of their ideas about the Americas from the not-always-accurate illustrations of Théodore de Bry, who worked in Germany in the mid-1500s. This illustration shows Indians collecting gold from a stream in the Appalachian Mountains.

as the Columbia and Snake. To the south lived the Great Basin peoples, who gathered berries, nuts, roots, and small game. The California culture group was highly diverse—some tribes fished, others wandered in search of wild foods. In the Southwestern culture group, the Hopi, Zuni, and Pueblo were farmers. The Navajo and Apache, who moved into that region in the 1500s, were hunters.

The Plains peoples were big-game hunters who stalked bison (buffalo) across the grasslands. The Southeast was home to farming peoples who grew tobacco, squash, and corn. In the north, the nations of the Eastern Woodlands also farmed, but they relied heavily on hunting and fishing as well. Many eastern tribes developed complex political systems and governments.

For thousands of years the first Americans had lived apart from the rest of the world. They had populated a continent and created a rich variety of cultures, languages, and beliefs. But newcomers from the outside were about to change the Native American world forever.

Chapter Two

EXPLORERS BY SEA

The first explorers of North America had come by land from Asia. The next wave of explorers came thousands of years later, from the opposite direction, and by sea.

The Vikings

The Vikings were seafaring raiders and traders from Norway and Sweden. In the 800s and 900s they were Europe's finest seamen. They crossed the stormy North Atlantic, establishing colonies on Iceland and other islands. In 982 they reached Greenland, the huge island that lies between Canada and Iceland in the far north. In a few sheltered spots on Greenland's southwestern coast, they founded small settlements.

Leif Eriksson was the son of the Viking who had founded the first Greenland settlement. Around 1001 he and thirty-five followers sailed

Leif Eriksson and his men approach the shore of Vinland—wherever it was. Although the Vikings failed to settle Vinland, they maintained a well-documented settlement in Greenland until sometime in the fifteenth century.

*Ptolemy, a Greek geographer who worked in Egypt during the second century A.D., created
a world map that European geographers copied hundreds of years later. This version of the Ptolemaic
world map was published in Ulm, Germany, in 1496. It repeats Ptolemy's view of the Indian Ocean—
the "Mare Indicum" on the map—as part of a landlocked sea, even though Bartolomeu Dias
of Portugal had already proved Ptolemy wrong by sailing around the southern tip
of Africa. Ptolemy's view of the world was simply too familiar to be easily overturned.*

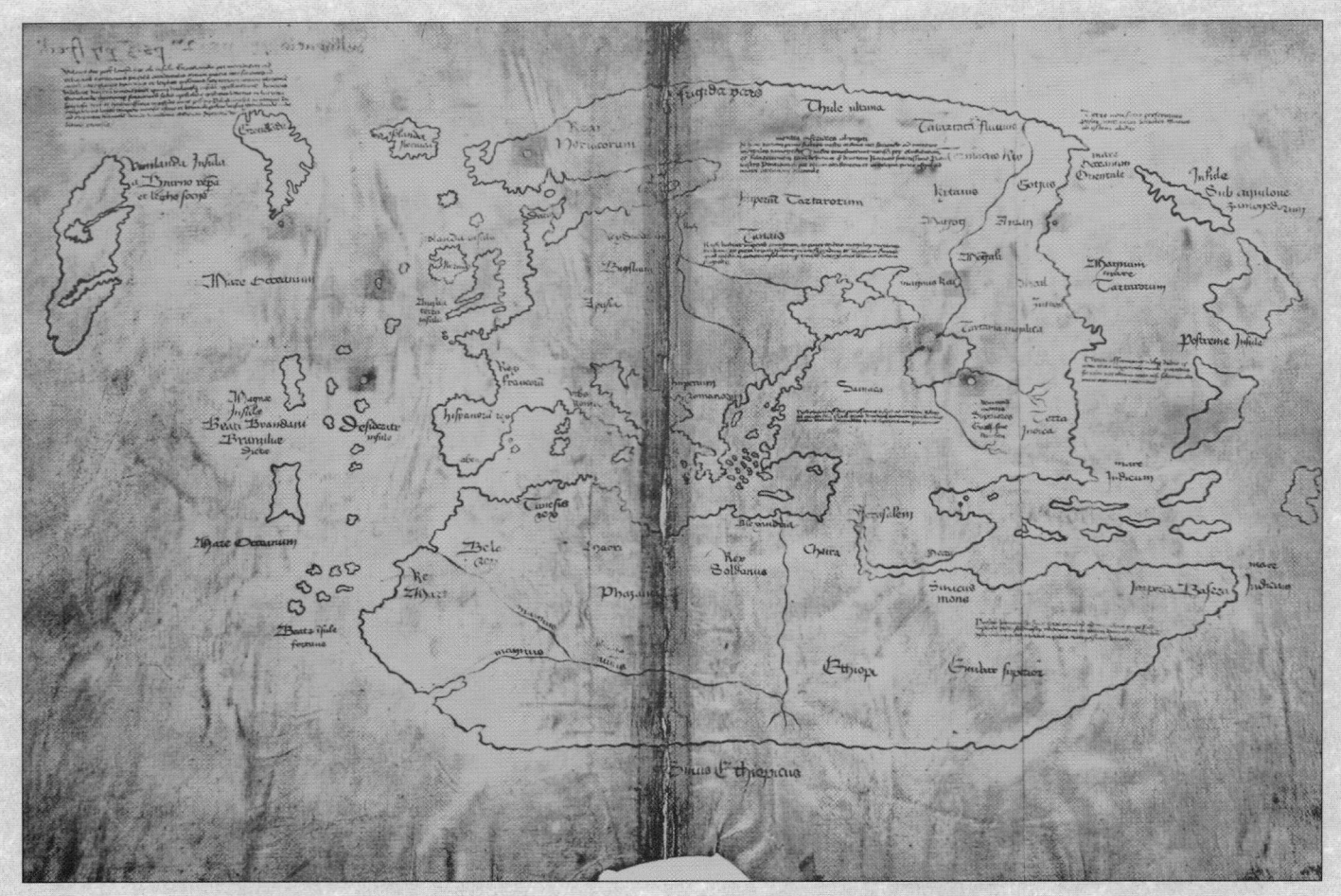

*Ever since the Vinland map was "discovered" in 1957, experts have
argued about it. It appears to date from around 1440, before Columbus's
voyages of discovery. Amazingly, however, it shows Vinland (in the upper left),
where the Vikings landed in North America around 1000. If it were genuine,
the Vinland map would be the oldest known European map to show
the Americas—but scientific examinations, such as chemical tests of the ink,
indicate that it is almost certainly a modern forgery. Even if authentic,
it still doesn't settle the question of Vinland's location.*

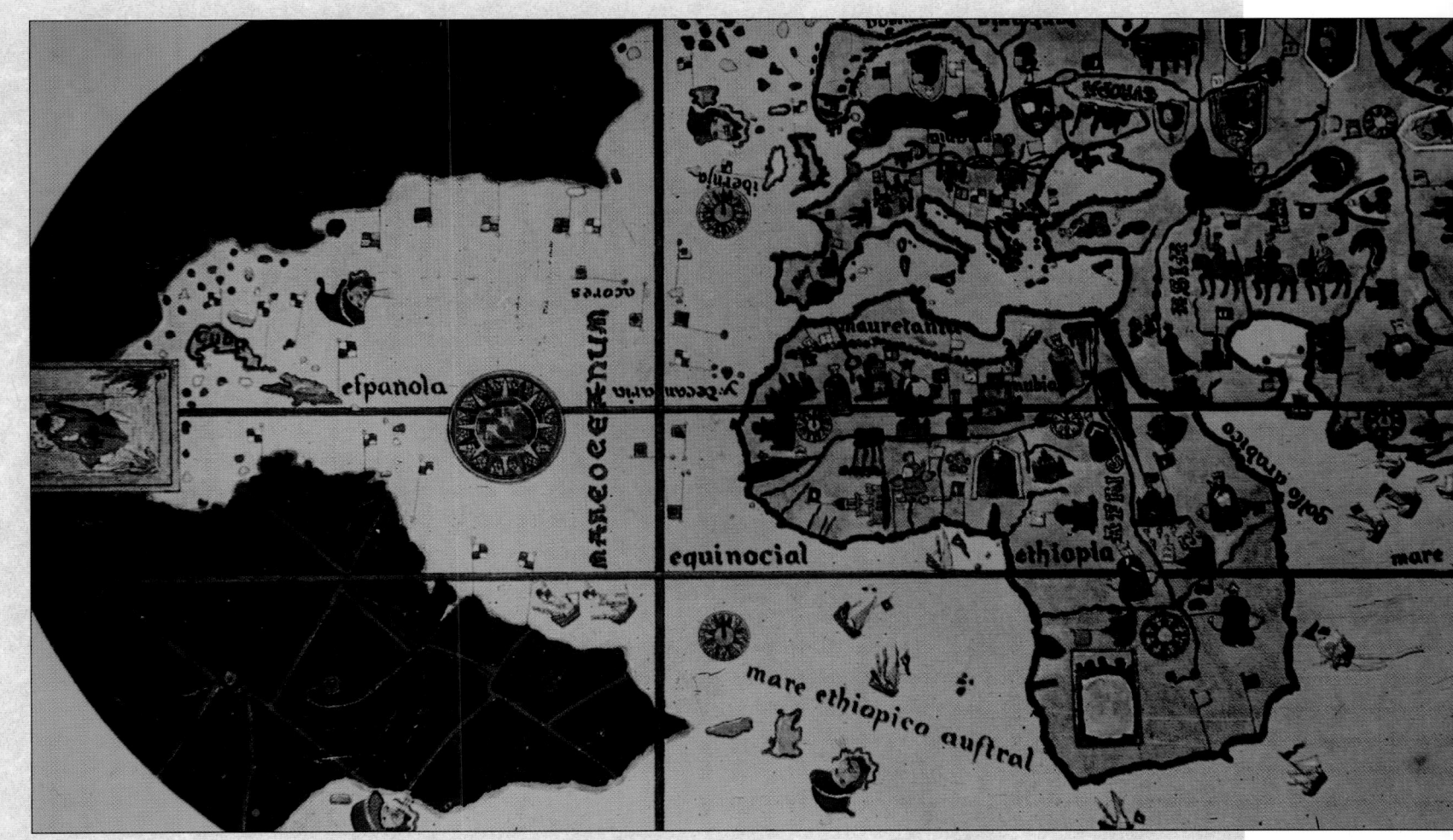

The first known world map to show the Americas. Juan de la Cosa, who sailed with Columbus, painted it on oxhide in 1500. The dark mass to the left is North and South America. "Espanola" is Hispaniola, Spain's first Caribbean colony, with Cuba above it.

west, looking for lands that other sailors had sighted in the distance. They would be the first Europeans to set foot in North America.

"Leif the Lucky," as some Norse tales call him, landed in three places. The first he called Helluland, "land of flat stones." The second he called Markland, "wooded land." The third he called Vinland, "wine land" or "vine land." Few questions in American history have aroused as much passion as the location of Vinland, but today most experts agree that it was probably the northern tip of Newfoundland Island. There, in 1961, researchers found remains of a 900-year-old Viking settlement—perhaps the very buildings where Leif and his men spent the winter of 1001 before returning to Greenland.

The Vikings made a few more visits to Vinland to cut timber, but they failed to start a permanent settlement there, partly because of fights with the local Native Americans. Soon the Viking adventure in North America ended. The next Europeans to arrive would not give up so easily.

Columbus Sails West to Reach the East

Christopher Columbus was not trying to reach America. He did not even know that it existed —the old tales of Vinland were unknown to most Europeans. Like many other Europeans in the 1400s, Columbus wanted to find a sea route to "the **Indies**," by which they meant India and the lands east and south of it. The Indies were the source of highly desirable spices, silk, and pearls. Europeans wanted to sail directly to the markets of the Indies instead of buying goods that traveled overland along lengthy, costly, and uncertain **caravan** routes.

The Portuguese had spent many years exploring the African coast, hoping to find a sea route to the east at the bottom of Africa. Columbus had a different idea. He knew that the world was round, and he figured that if he sailed far enough west, he would come upon the Indies from the other side. His idea was brilliant, with only two problems. First, Columbus did not know how *far* west he would have to sail. And second, he was completely unaware that the Americas and the Pacific Ocean lay in his way.

With backing from Spain, Columbus set sail in 1492. After five weeks he arrived at a low-lying island in warm blue water. Thinking he had reached the Indies, he called the local people Indians. He was disappointed, however, to find no trace of the bustling cities, prosperous markets, or splendid courts that Marco Polo and other overland travelers to Asia had described.

Columbus tried again the next year. This time he set up a **colony** on the Caribbean island of Hispaniola—the first permanent European outpost in the New World. But Columbus did not know that it was a "new world." He insisted that he had reached the Indies, and he kept on insisting until King Ferdinand and Queen Isabella of Spain agreed to pay for a third voyage in 1498. Columbus still could not find the rich ports of the Indies. To make matters worse, he got into trouble for mismanaging the Hispaniola colony and was sent back to Spain in disgrace—and in chains.

THE EDGE OF THE WORLD

Schoolchildren once learned that Columbus's men, believing the earth to be flat, feared they would sail over its edge. This was a myth. Most seamen of Columbus's day, like most educated people, knew perfectly well that the earth was round. They just did not know how big it was.

Columbus's men did indeed fear that their commander was leading them into danger. They were not afraid of falling off the edge of the world, but they *were* afraid that they had gone so far that they might not be able to make their way home, especially with winds and currents against them. To calm their grumblings, Columbus fiddled with the figures in the ship's log, making it appear that the fleet had covered a shorter distance than was really the case.

Christopher Columbus's three ships—the Niña, Pinta, *and* Santa Maria*— were caravels, a type of vessel that was small, nimble, and easy to steer. Developed in Portugal in the early fifteenth century, the caravel was a huge step forward in European ocean voyaging.*

Christopher Columbus was perhaps the luckiest and the unluckiest of the European explorers in North America. He was lucky because, after years of effort, he persuaded the king and queen of Spain to sponsor his voyages—and also because he survived a crossing that was much longer than he had expected. Unluckily, Columbus never did reach Asia, his goal. So determined was he to prove that he had reached the Indies, however, that on his second voyage he forced his crew to sign an oath that they believed Cuba to be part of Asia. All signed, and no wonder—Columbus had threatened to cut out the tongue of anyone who refused.

THE FOUR VOYAGES OF CHRISTOPHER COLUMBUS

— 1st Voyage 1492
— 2nd Voyage 1493
— 3rd Voyage 1498
— 4th Voyage 1502

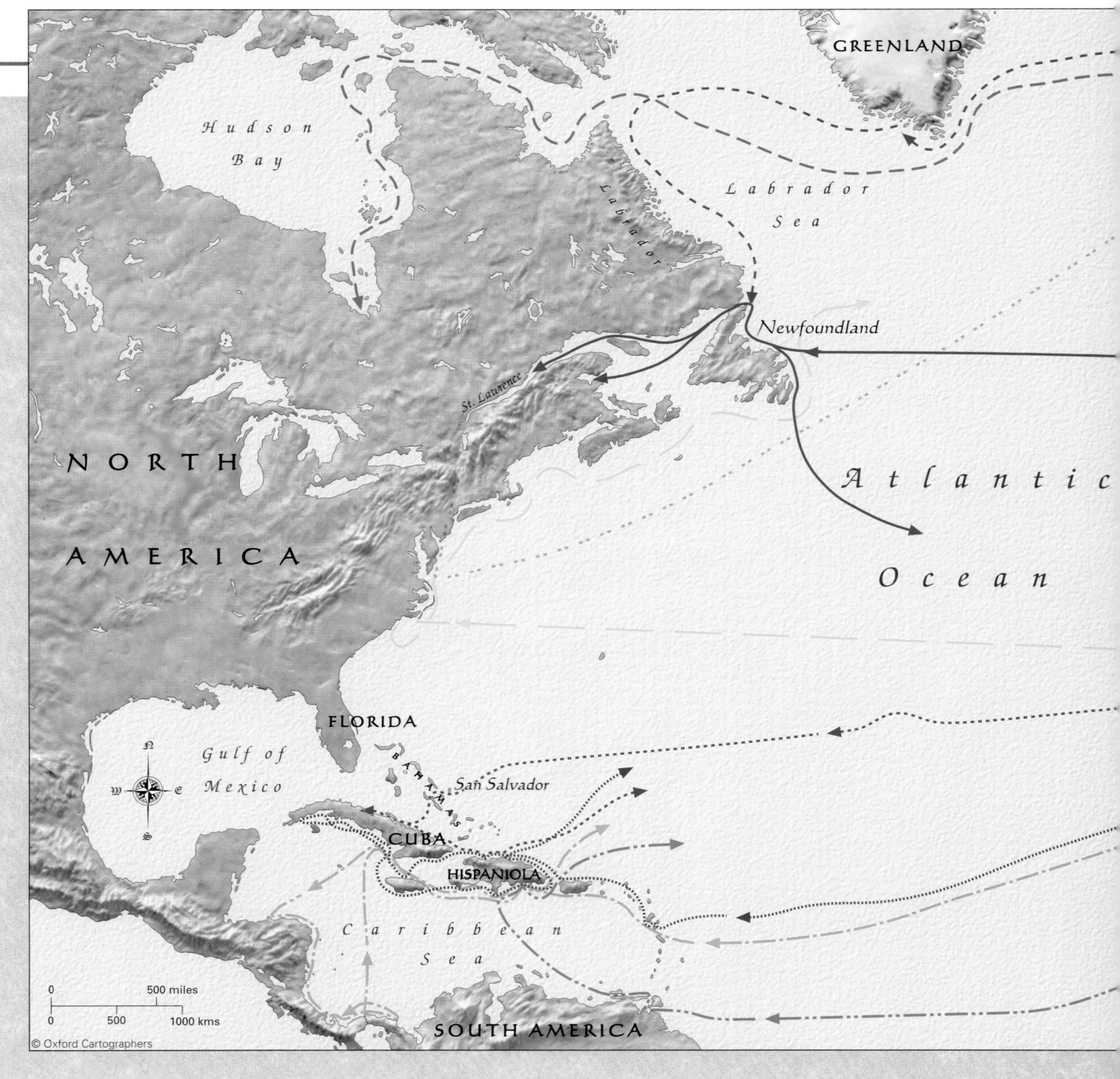

GREENLAND

Hudson Bay

Labrador Sea

Labrador

Newfoundland

St. Lawrence

NORTH AMERICA

Atlantic Ocean

Gulf of Mexico

FLORIDA

BAHAMAS

San Salvador

CUBA

HISPANIOLA

Caribbean Sea

SOUTH AMERICA

N
W E
S

0   500 miles
0   500   1000 kms

© Oxford Cartographers

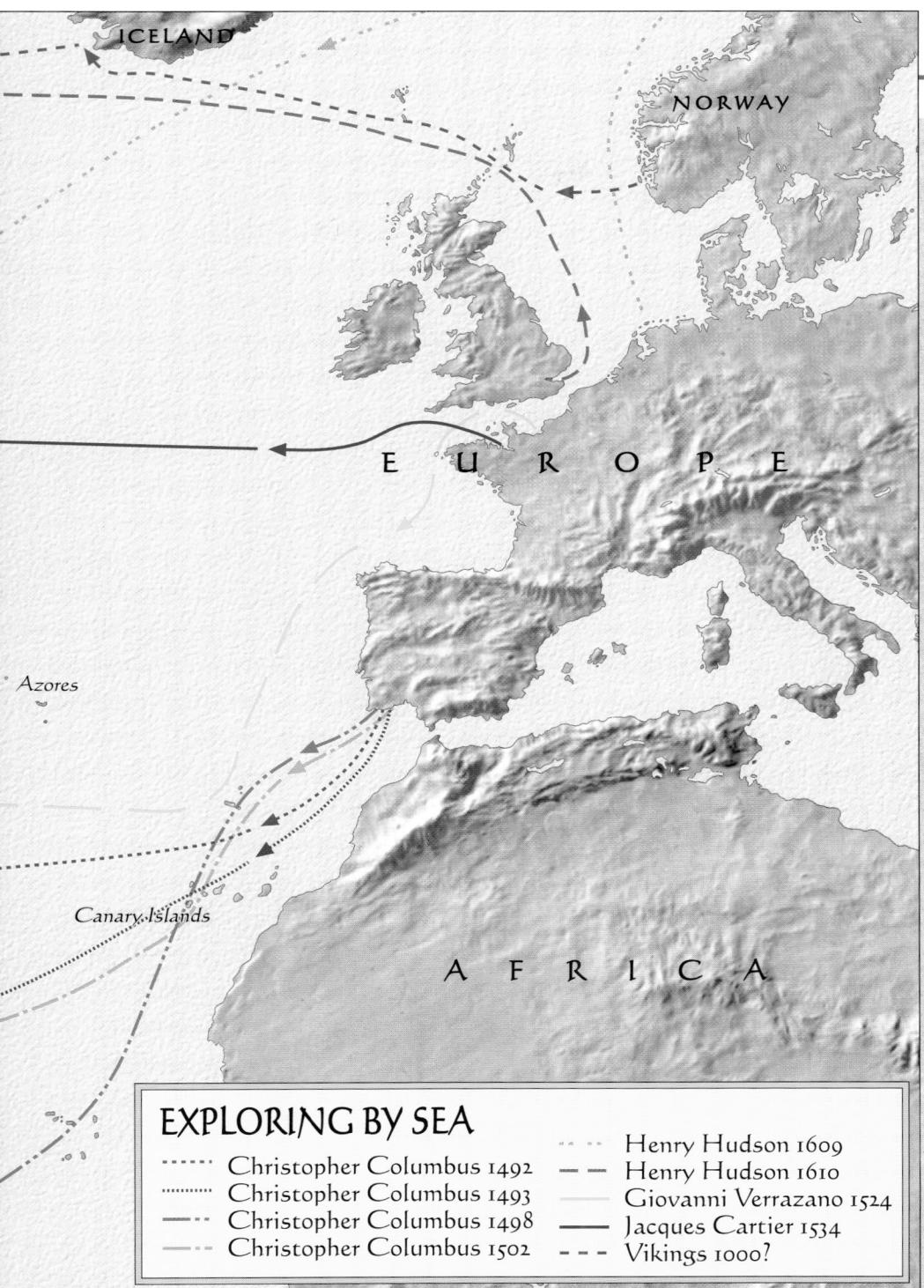

ICELAND

NORWAY

EUROPE

Azores

Canary Islands

AFRICA

EXPLORING BY SEA

- ····· Christopher Columbus 1492
- ········· Christopher Columbus 1493
- —·· Christopher Columbus 1498
- —··· Christopher Columbus 1502
- ····· Henry Hudson 1609
- — — Henry Hudson 1610
- —— Giovanni Verrazano 1524
- —— Jacques Cartier 1534
- — — Vikings 1000?

The seaports of western Europe were the jumping-off points for voyages westward, first into the unknown and then to what Europeans called "the New World," the Americas. Venturing across the Atlantic Ocean was no easy feat. Crossings took from five to twelve weeks, depending upon wind and weather. As travel back and forth between Europe and North America increased, navigators discovered that the Atlantic Ocean contains powerful currents, and they learned to shorten their voyages by "riding" westward-flowing currents to the Caribbean and eastward-flowing ones, such as the Gulf Stream, back to Europe.

German mapmaker Sebastian Munster followed the European tradition of decorating unknown areas with pictures. In Brazil he drew a structure from which hang a severed human head and a leg, reflecting explorers' reports of cannibals in the region. He also greatly underestimated the size of North America.

The king and queen gave Columbus one final chance, and in 1502 he made his fourth and last voyage west. Again failing to find the route to the Indies, he returned to Spain. He died in 1506, disappointed but still stubbornly insisting that he had reached Asia.

The Discovery of Florida

Even before Columbus's death other explorers had realized that the western lands were not part of Asia. Soon the "New World" came to be known as the Americas. Europeans set about probing its mysteries—and helping themselves to whatever riches it contained.

Not all riches were of gold or silver. A rumor arose that somewhere to the north was a "fountain of youth." Those who drank of its waters never aged or fell ill. Juan Ponce de León, who had come to the Americas with Columbus's second voyage and served briefly as the governor of Puerto Rico, believed in those tales. In 1513 he set off to find the miraculous fountain.

Ponce de León sighted an unknown coast and named it Florida. He explored its eastern and western coasts but found no fountain—only swamps, snakes, alligators, and hostile Indians. In 1521 he returned to Florida to build a colony there, but died of a wound he had received in a fight with the local Native Americans. Florida *did* become a Spanish colony, however, and the city of St. Augustine, the oldest continuously occupied European settlement in North America, rose where Ponce de León first landed.

Mapping the Atlantic Coast

France challenged Spain's claim to the new western lands. In 1524 the French king sent an Italian navigator named Giovanni Verrazano to probe the American coastline north of the Spanish colonies, looking for a passage to Asia. Verrazano did not find such a passage, but he did explore the eastern coast of North America from the Carolinas to Maine.

Verrazano's voyage brought a new understanding of North American geography. He proved that North America was not, as some believed, a series of islands, but rather a continuous coastline. He also discovered what is now New York Harbor. Yet Verrazano made one big mistake. He thought the islands of Carolina's Outer Banks were a narrow strip of land with the Pacific Ocean west of them. Verrazano's brother drew a map that showed the Pacific practically cutting North America in two above Florida—an error that appeared on maps for nearly one hundred years.

Into Canada

France's second major exploration of the New World took place in the mid-1530s under Jacques Cartier. Like Verrazano, Cartier was not really trying to explore North America— he was looking for a route *through* it to Asia.

Cartier sailed up the St. Lawrence River as far as the present site of Quebec City, then pushed on to the place where Montreal now stands. Prevented by rapids from going farther, Cartier learned from local Indians of other rivers to the west. Perhaps one of them was the long-sought passage to the Pacific? Alas,

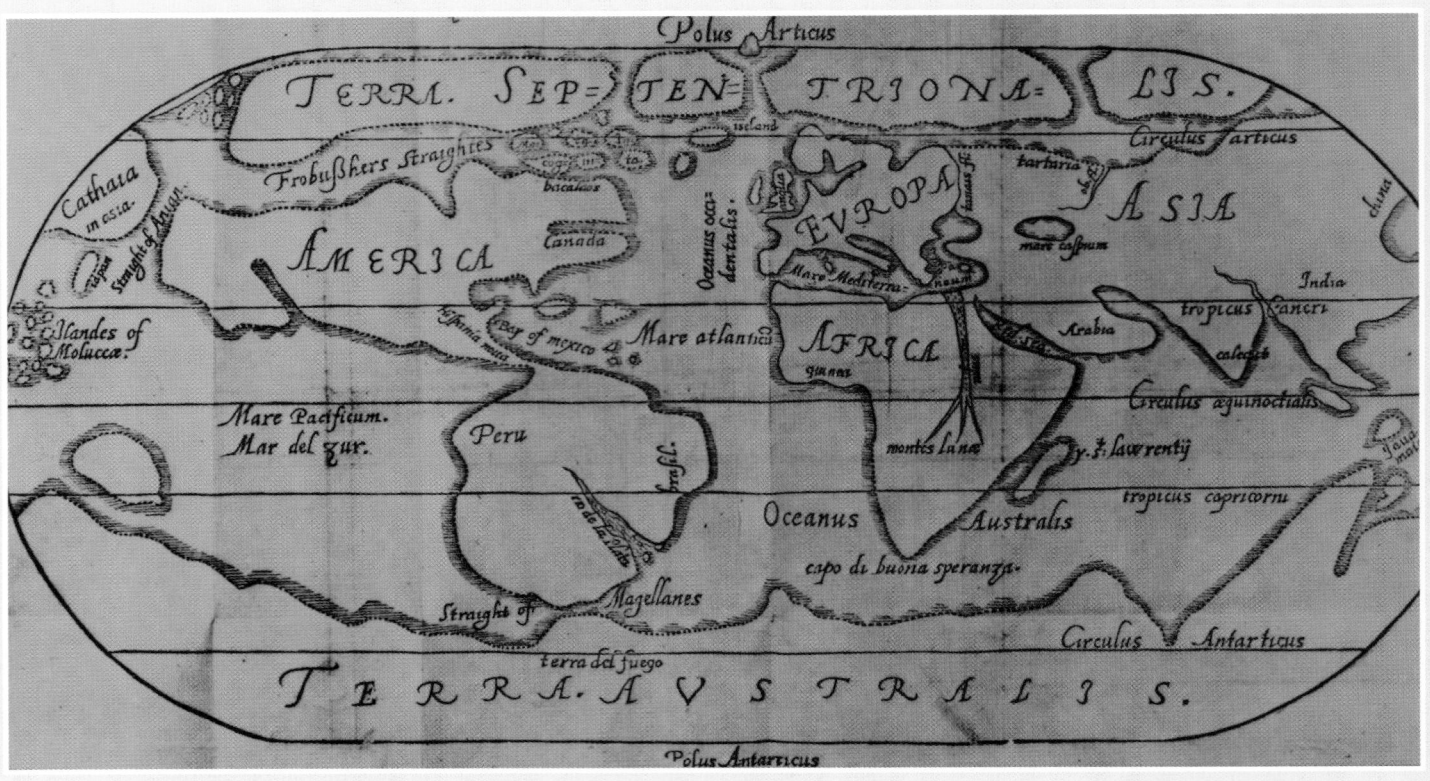

George Best, a shipmate of Martin Frobisher, said that Frobisher believed that finding the Northwest Passage was the only feat "whereby a notable mind might be made famous and fortunate." Frobisher failed to find the nonexistent passage. That didn't stop Best from making this map showing a wide, straight Northwest Passage—labeled "Frobishers Straightes" in honor of his friend—leading directly to China ("Cathaia").

 European explorers spent centuries searching for a water route through or around North America to the Indies. Many pinned their hopes on what they called the **Northwest Passage**, a westward-leading waterway thought to lie somewhere in the northern part of the continent. Every time a sea captain sighted a river mouth,

bay, or inlet, hope flared anew—maybe *this* was the Passage at last!

English navigators Martin Frobisher (1570s) and John Davis (1580s) were just two of many who searched for the Passage in the ice-choked seas of the Canadian Arctic. Luckier than some, they survived. In the 1840s Sir John Franklin and his entire expedition died trying to find the Passage in the Canadian Arctic. The search parties that looked for Franklin mapped the region and proved that the only Northwest Passage that existed was too dangerous and too far north to be useful for shipping.

Martin Frobisher of England was one of the first Europeans to venture into the forbidding, ice-clogged Arctic waterways in search of the Northwest Passage. This image of Inuit (formerly called Eskimo) life appeared in a 1580 account of his voyages.

JACQUES CARTIER 1491–1557

Jacques Cartier's voyages bitterly disappointed his royal French sponsors. Not only did Cartier fail to find a Northwest Passage through North America, he found no gold or gems. He did, however, stake France's claim to what would one day be a huge colony in Canada.

Cartier was not to find out. He and his men spent a horrible winter in Canada, suffering from the bitter cold and the lack of fresh food. Several dozen crew members died. When the river thawed in the spring, the survivors gratefully set sail for France.

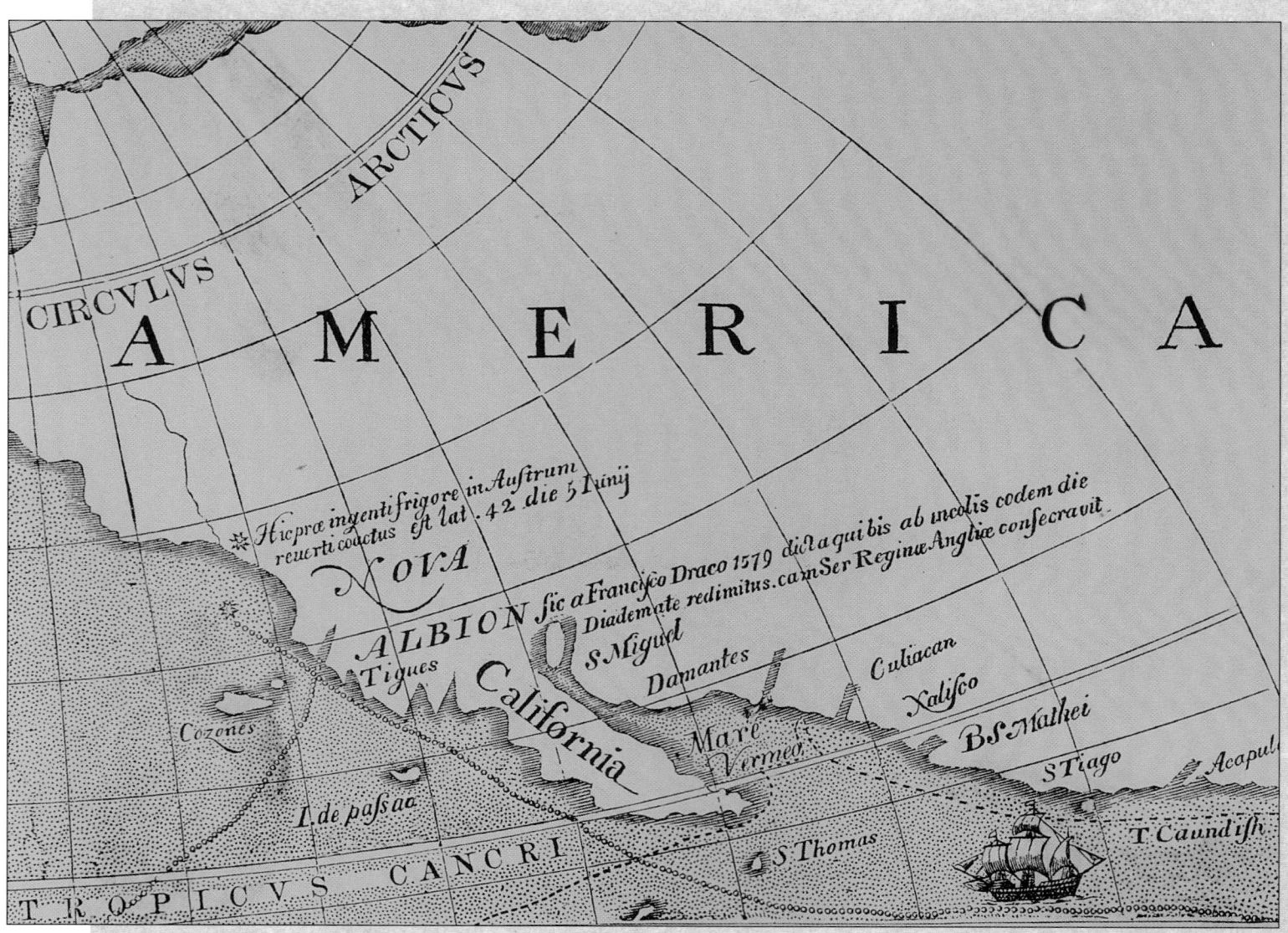

Around 1600 a Dutch mapmaker published this map of Sir Francis Drake's voyage along the west coast of North America, which he claimed for England. If the English had acted on Drake's claim and established colonies north of Spanish Mexico, the term "New England" would now refer to California, not to the area around Massachusetts.

In 1541 Cartier made a last journey to Canada, collecting rocks that he thought contained a fortune in gold and diamonds. Back in France, however, the rocks proved to be worthless. It was fifty years before the French showed any more interest in Canada, but Cartier's voyages had laid the basis for a long-lasting French claim.

First Claim to California

England's Sir Francis Drake was a **privateer**, a sea captain who had his ruler's permission to attack the ships and ports of England's enemies. Spain was an enemy, and during the 1570s and 1580s Drake terrorized Spanish shipping and Spanish colonies in the New World.

In 1579, during a voyage around the world, Drake sailed along the west coast of North America, searching for a waterway that would lead him east. He explored several likely looking possibilities, including the large bay where San Francisco now stands. Somewhere near that bay he claimed the land for England and named it New Albion (an old name for England) before continuing his voyage. No one is certain exactly where Drake went ashore to make that claim, and, in any event, England never established a colony in California, which instead fell into Spanish hands.

Chapter Three

EXPLORERS
BY LAND

Once explorers had traced parts of the North American coastline, they moved inland. It would take many years—and many difficult journeys—to complete the mapping of North America's vast interior.

Exploration and Conquest

The first Spanish explorers of the interior were the **conquistadors**, or military leaders, who came to conquer the land as well as explore it. They won control of Mexico and then looked to the rest of the Americas. One of them, Hernando de Soto, cut a bloody path through southeastern North America between 1539 and 1542.

Soto and his band marched north from Florida and then followed a rambling route through Georgia, South Carolina, Tennessee, Alabama, Arkansas, Mississippi, and Louisiana. They were searching for rich kingdoms like those the Spanish had conquered in Mexico and Peru, but they found only Native American communities that they attacked and plundered. Their repeated outrages earned the hatred of the Indians, who began attacking the marchers. The brutal expedition ended when Soto died of a fever and his surviving followers made their way to Spanish Mexico.

A Conquistador in Kansas

Rumors of large Indian towns north of Mexico and the Spanish lust for gold combined to create the legend of the Seven Cities of Cibola. These cities were said to be rich beyond compare, with walls of gold. In 1538 a Spanish **friar** set off from Mexico to find them, with Esteban—a survivor of the wrecked 1528 expedition—as his guide. Indians killed Esteban, but the friar returned to Mexico claiming that the golden cities really did exist. Two years later he accompanied the large, well-equipped

ON FOOT TO MEXICO

 In 1536 four men arrived in Mexico after a long journey. Three were Spanish. The other, called Esteban or Estenbanico, was an African slave—the first known black explorer of North America. They were survivors of a Spanish expedition that in 1528 had set out to explore the northern coast of the Gulf of Mexico. Indian attacks and shipwreck had destroyed the expedition. The leader of the survivors, Alvar Nuñez Cabeza de Vaca, had won the friendship of Native Americans who fed the four men and guided them from Texas to Mexico City. Some 600 Indians, in fact, were so impressed with Cabeza de Vaca that they followed him all the way to Mexico.

expedition of Francisco Vázquez de Coronado north to look for them.

When the "golden cities" turned out to be adobe-walled Indian villages, many of the conquistadors hurled bitter curses at the friar. Still, Coronado pressed on in a quest that eventually carried him as far north and east as Kansas. His return to Mexico with no gold or silver to show for his efforts made him unpopular with Spanish officials. His expedition did, however, discover one shining treasure—the immense rift in the Earth that we now call the Grand Canyon.

The Southwest

Half a century after Coronado, the Spanish had given up the idea of finding golden cities in the Southwest. But they still wanted to explore and settle the region on the northern frontier of the vast colony called New Spain. Juan de Oñate was the most vigorous investigator of the Southwest in the late 1500s and early 1600s.

Hernando de Soto's three-year expedition into the interior of the Southeast was a disaster—especially for the Native Americans he brutalized. A Spanish historian wrote at the time that Soto had "caused alteration and desolation of the land and loss of liberty of people, without making Christians or friends."

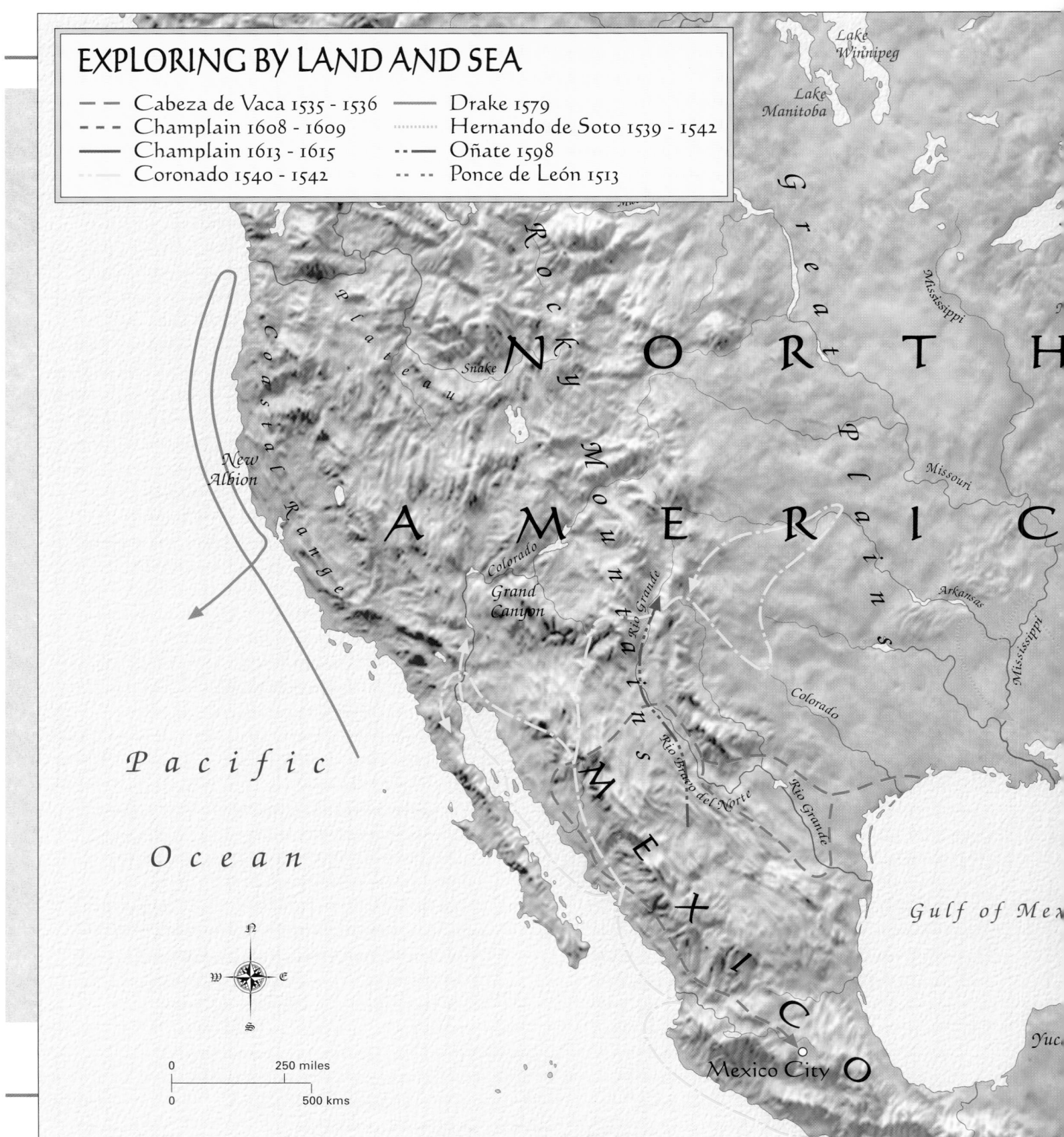

EXPLORING BY LAND AND SEA

- – – Cabeza de Vaca 1535 – 1536
- – – – Champlain 1608 – 1609
- —— Champlain 1613 – 1615
- – · – Coronado 1540 – 1542
- —— Drake 1579
- ·········· Hernando de Soto 1539 – 1542
- – · – Oñate 1598
- – · – Ponce de León 1513

Lake Winnipeg

Lake Manitoba

Rocky

Great

N O R T H

Mississippi

Plateau

Snake

Plains

Missouri

A M E R I C A

New Albion

Coastal Range

M o u n t a i n s

Colorado

Grand Canyon

Rio Grande

Arkansas

Mississippi

Colorado

Rio Grande

M E X I C O

Río Bravo del Norte

Rio Grande

P a c i f i c

O c e a n

Gulf of Mex

Yuca

Mexico City ⊙

N
W E
S

| 0 | | 250 miles |
| 0 | | 500 kms |

Not until several hundred years after Columbus did Europeans fully realize just how large North America was. The size of the continent, together with resistance from some Native Americans and an often forbidding terrain that included swamps, mountains, and deserts, kept the first explorers from probing very far inland from the coasts. Although the exploration of North America's vast interior began in the early sixteenth century with the expeditions shown on this map, it would not really be completed until the late nineteenth century, when American explorers finally charted the remote river canyons and plateaus of the Rocky Mountains and the Southwest.

American artist Frederic Remington, known for his paintings and sculptures of Western subjects, depicted Francisco Vázquez de Coronado's men pursuing phantom riches across the sun-baked deserts of the Southwest.

Inheritor of a huge fortune from Mexican silver mines, Oñate was assigned by the Spanish crown to conquer and colonize what is now New Mexico. In 1598 he established the first settlement there. From this base he explored the harsh landscape of valleys and deserts as far west as the Gulf of California at the mouth of the Colorado River.

From Exploration to Settlement

In 1604 French explorer Samuel de Champlain started a settlement in Canada, but difficult conditions forced the settlers to abandon the colony after a few years. Champlain tried

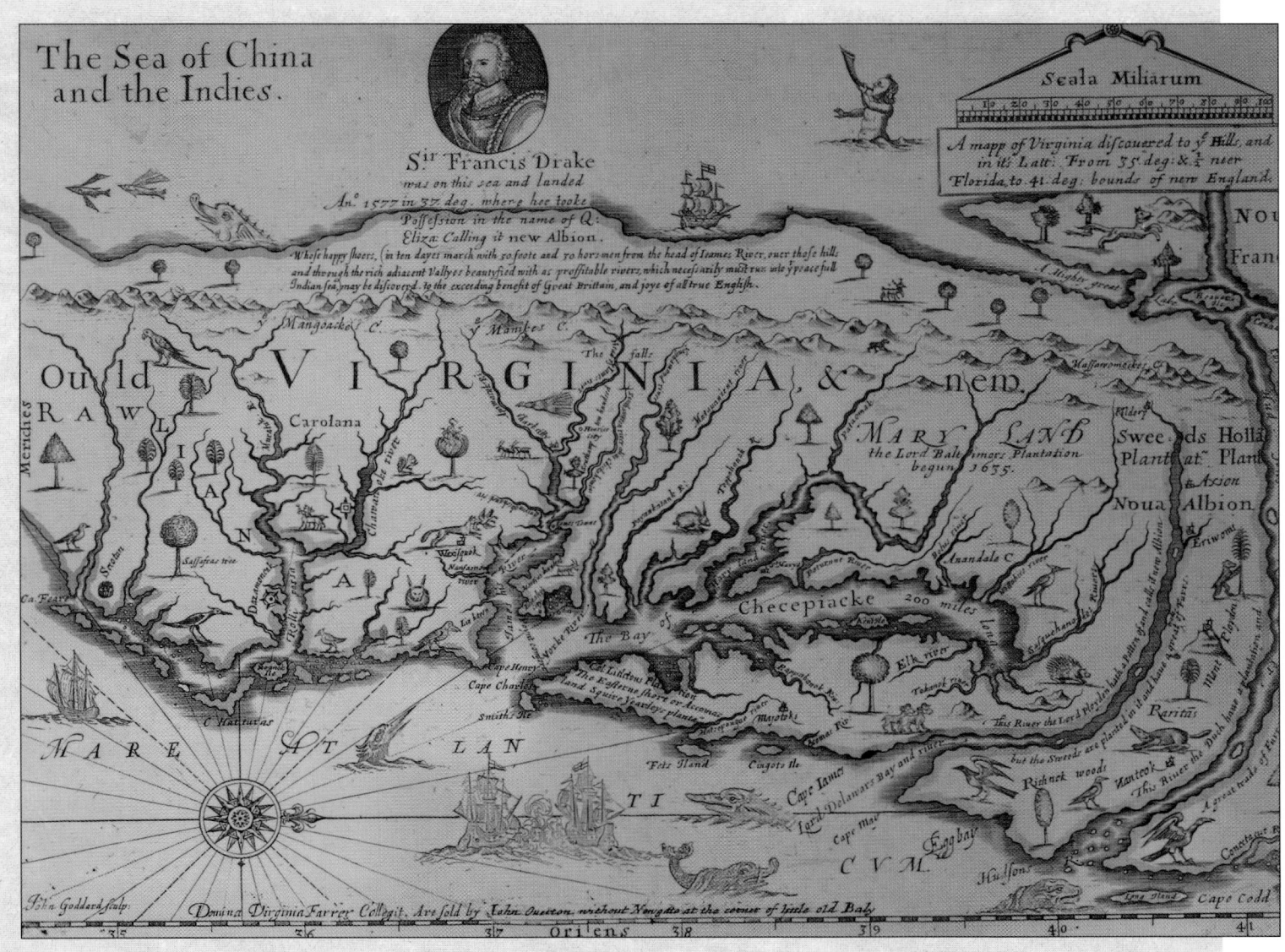

The following text labels appear on the map:

The Sea of China and the Indies.

Sir Francis Drake
was on this sea and landed
An.° 1577 in 37 deg. where hee tooke
Possession in the name of Q:
Eliza: Calling it new Albion.
Whose happy shoers, (in ten dayes march with 50 foote and 30 horsmen from the head of Iames River, over those hills
and through the rich adiacent Vallyes beautyfied with as profitable rivers, which necessarily must run into y.e pace full
Indian sea, may be discovered to the exceeding benefit of Great Brittain, and joye of all true English.

Scala Miliarum

A mapp of Virginia discovered to y.e Hills, and
in it's Latt: From 35. deg: & ¼ neer
Florida, to 41. deg: bounds of new England.

Ould VIRGINIA, & new.

RAWLIANA

Carolana

MARY LAND
the Lord Baltimors Plantation
begun 1635.

Sweeds Holla
Plant at Plant

Noua Albion

Checepiacke

200 miles

The Bay

Cape Henry
Cape Charles

Smiths Ile

C. Fear

MARE ATLANTI CVM

Oriens

John Goddard sculp.

Domina Virginia Farrer Collegit. Are sold by John Ouerton, without Newgate at the corner of little old Bayly

A fanciful early map of Virginia and the other English colonies in North America
shows how little mapmakers knew about the true size of the continent—Drake's landfall
on the Pacific Ocean (at the top of the map) seems to lie just beyond the hills in back
of the settlements. Wild animals and fish frolic in the map's empty spaces.

ROANOKE ISLAND

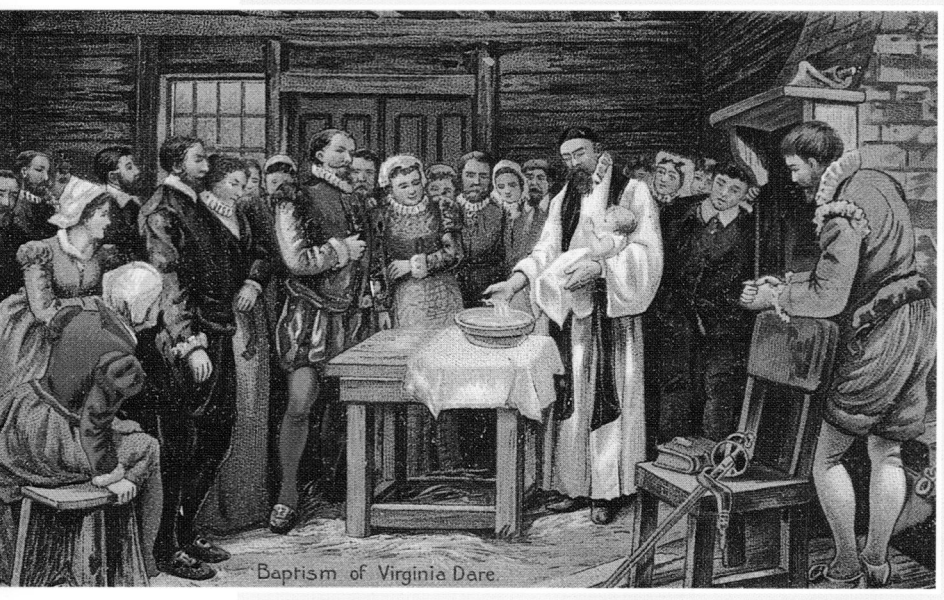

Baptism of Virginia Dare.

The Roanoke colonists may have celebrated at the baptism of Virginia Dare, but soon all of them—including Virginia—would disappear without a trace.

 Exploration led to settlement attempts. Some of these attempts failed. One failure—and a lasting mystery—involved Roanoke Island, off the coast of North Carolina. In 1585 England's Sir Walter Raleigh sent one hundred men to found a colony there. Unhappy, the settlers returned to England. Several years later Raleigh tried again with a group of ninety-one men, seven-teen women, and nine children under John White's command. After sailing back to England for supplies and more settlers, White found himself unable to return at once to Roanoke. Three years later, when he finally made it back to the island, the colony had vanished— including his granddaughter Virginia Dare, the first English child born in North America. The fate of the colonists remains unknown, although they may have moved to another island about 100 miles (161 kilometers) away. Nobody was ever seen again.

Sir Walter Raleigh, founder of Roanoke, also explored South America in search of El Dorado, a fabled city of gold. He didn't find it, but he wrote a wildly exaggerated and romantic book about his adventures.

The founder of New France, Samuel de Champlain, drew this map of the colony in eastern Canada. Note the accurate placement of such details as Quebec on the St. Lawrence River and Lake Champlain in what is now New York.

again in 1608, establishing a successful settlement in Quebec. It became the center of France's North American empire.

Far to the south, on the Virginia coast, a group of English colonists had established a settlement called Jamestown in 1607. Although hunger and fighting with the Indians nearly destroyed the colony, it managed to survive—and even to make money by growing tobacco for sale in England. Although much exploration remained to be done, the colonization of North America was under way.

Glossary

archaeologist: A type of scientist who studies past cultures and civilizations.

caravan: A group of people and pack animals traveling overland together, usually carrying trade goods.

colony: A territory outside the borders of a state but claimed or controlled by that state.

conquistador: A Spanish military leader involved in the exploration of the Americas and the conquest of the Native American peoples.

friar: A member of a religious brotherhood.

geologist: A type of scientist who studies the earth and its features.

glacier: A large, slowly moving "river" or sheet of ice, today found only in mountains.

Indies: A European term for India, southeast Asia, and eastern Asia; source of the name "Indians" for the Native Americans, whom Columbus believed to be Asians.

irrigation: Using manmade structures such as ditches and dams to bring water to dry fields.

mammoth: A prehistoric mammal that ate plants and had long tusks. The mammoth was similar in appearance to the modern elephant but was covered with shaggy hair.

Northwest Passage: The water route that Europeans hoped to find through North America from the Atlantic Ocean to the Pacific.

privateer: A ship's owner or captain who has permission from the ruler of his nation to attack ships of enemy nations.

settlement: A permanent or long-lasting home for a group of people.

steppe-tundra: Northern landscape that combines steppes (treeless grasslands) and tundra (places where the soil below the surface remains frozen all year, often marshy in summer).

Map List

ABOUT THE HISTORICAL MAPS

The historical maps used in this book are primary source documents found in the following collections.

Map of Vinland: The Beinecke Rare Book and Manuscript Library at Yale University.

George Best's World Map: Rare Books Division, The New York Public Library, Astor, Lenox, and Tilden Collections.

Samuel de Champlain's map of eastern Canada: Rare Books Division, The New York Public Library, Astor, Lenox, and Tilden Collections.

Map of Virginia: The Library of Congress Maps Division.

Chronology

BEFORE 15,000 YEARS AGO   A land bridge links Asia and North America. Asian hunters cross it into Alaska. They are the ancestors of the Native Americans.

9500-9000 B.C.   The Paleoindian Clovis culture flourishes on the plains.

AROUND A.D. 1000   Vikings from Greenland visit the northeastern coast of North America.

1492-1493   Christopher Columbus makes his first voyage from Spain to North America.

1513   Juan Ponce de León explores the Florida coast.

1524   Giovanni Verrazano maps the east coast.

1534-1536   Jacques Cartier of France begins the exploration of Canada.

1539-1542   Hernando de Soto leads a Spanish expedition into the Southeast.

1541   Francisco Vázquez de Coronado searches for legendary cities in the Southwest.

1579   Francis Drake claims California for England.

1598   Juan de Oñate founds a Spanish settlement in New Mexico.

EARLY 1600s   The English (1607) and French (1608) establish their first successful settlements in North America.

Further Reading

Brown, Warren. *The Search for the Northwest Passage.* New York: Chelsea House Publishers, 1991.

Goetzmann, William H. and Glyndwr Williams. *The Atlas of North American Exploration.* Norman, OK: University of Oklahoma Press, 1998.

Hakim, Joy. *The First Americans.* New York: Oxford University Press, 1994.

Maestro, Guilio and Betsy C. Maestro. *Exploration and Conquest: The Americas After Columbus.* New York: Lothrop Lee & Shepard, 1994.

Morley, Jacqueline. *Exploring North America.* New York: Peter Bedrick Books, 1996.
Stefoff, Rebecca. *The Viking Explorers.* New York: Chelsea House Publishers, 1993.

Wilbur, C. Keith. *Early Explorers of North America.* Old Saybrook, CT: Globe Pequot Press, 1996.

WEBSITES

The Library of Congress Geography and Maps: An Illustrated Guide
www.loc.gov/rr/geogmap/guide

Map History
www.maphist.nl

Map Societies
www.csuohio.edu/CUT/MapSoc/Name_indx.htm

ABOUT THE AUTHOR

Rebecca Stefoff is the author of numerous books for children and young adults. Many of them deal with the history of exploration. Among these are her three-volume Extraordinary Explorers series, published in 1992 by Oxford University Press: *Accidental Explorers, Women of the World,* and *Scientific Explorers.* She makes her home in Portland, Oregon.

Index

Entries are filed letter-by-letter. Page numbers for illustrations and maps are in boldface.